# WILD WICKED WONDERFUL

# TOP 10:

# STINKERS

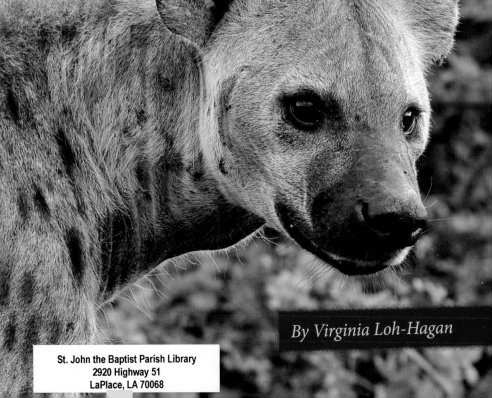

By Virginia Loh-Hagan

 45th Parallel Press

Published in the United States of America by Cherry Lake Publishing
Ann Arbor, Michigan
www.cherrylakepublishing.com

Content Adviser: Stephen Ditchkoff, Professor of Wildlife Ecology and Management, Auburn University, Alabama
Reading Adviser: Marla Conn, ReadAbility, Inc.
Book Designer: Melinda Millward

Photo Credits: ©john michael evan potter/Shutterstock Images, cover, 1, 18; ©davemhuntphotography/Shutterstock Images, 5; ©Jason X Pacheco/Shutterstock Images, 6; ©Taiftin/Shutterstock Images, 6; ©Ingrid Prats/Shutterstock Images, 6; ©Carlesmayet/Dreamstime.com, 7; ©Dave Montreuil/Shutterstock Images, 8; © Matt Cuda/Dreamstime.com, 8; ©MattiaATH/Shutterstock Images, 8; ©Pal Teravagimov/Shutterstock Images, 9; ©Dennis W. Donohue/Shutterstock Images, 10; ©smileimage9/Shutterstock Images, 12; ©Anna Omelchenko/Shutterstock Images, 12; ©Sharon Haeger/Shutterstock Images, 12; ©Fiona Ayerst/Shutterstock Images, 13; ©Graeme Shannon/Shutterstock Images, 14; ©Alexey Stiop/Shutterstock Images, 16; © Tobias Bernhard Raff/Copyright : www.biosphoto.com/Biosphoto/Corbis, 17; © Mhpiper/Dreamstime.com, 18; ©apple2499/Shutterstock Images, 18; © Stefanie Van Der Vinden/Dreamstime.com, 19; ©Nicram Sabod/Shutterstock Images, 20; ©Wolfgang Kruck/Shutterstock Images, 20; © Kloeg008/Dreamstime.com, 21; ©Joakim Lloyd Raboff/Shutterstock Images, 22; ©David Steele/Shutterstock Images, 22; ©JONATHAN PLEDGER/Shutterstock Images, 22; ©jacotakepics/Shutterstock Images, 23; ©Ryan M. Bolton/Shutterstock Images, 24; ©Joy Stein/Shutterstock Images, 25; ©Stubblefield Photography/Shutterstock Images, 26; ©jo Crebbin/Shutterstock Images, 26; ©Dmytro Pylypenko/Shutterstock Images, 26; ©sAndrew M. Allport/Shutterstock Images, 27; ©James Coleman/Shutterstock Images, 28; ©Comstock Images /Thinkstock, 29; ©Critterbiz/Shutterstock Images, 30; ©Dennis Jacobsen/Shutterstock Images, 31

Graphic Element Credits: © tukkki/Shutterstock Images, back cover, front cover, multiple interior pages; © paprika/Shutterstock Images, back cover, front cover, multiple interior pages; © Silhouette Lover/Shutterstock Images, multiple interior pages

**45th Parallel Press** is an imprint of Cherry Lake Publishing.

Library of Congress Cataloging-in-Publication Data

Loh-Hagan, Virginia, author.
    Top 10 : stinkers / by Virginia Loh-Hagan.
pages cm. — (Wild wicked wonderful)
Summary: "Dive into the Wild Wicked Wonderful world of the animal kingdom with the Top 10: Stinkers. Written with a high interest level to appeal to a more mature audience and a lower level of complexity with clear visuals to help struggling readers along. Considerate text includes tons of fascinating information and wild facts that will hold the readers' interest, allowing for successful mastery and comprehension. A table of contents, glossary with simplified pronunciations, and index all enhance comprehension."— Provided by publisher.
ISBN 978-1-63470-506-6 (hardcover) — ISBN 978-1-63470-626-1 (pbk.) —
ISBN 978-1-63470-566-0 (pdf) — ISBN 978-1-63470-686-5 (ebook)
1. Animals—Miscellanea—Juvenile literature. I. Title. II. Title: Top ten : stinkers. III. Title: Stinkers.

QL49.L8355 2016
590—dc23          2015026858

Printed in the United States of America
Corporate Graphics

## About the Author

Dr. Virginia Loh-Hagan is an author, university professor, former classroom teacher, and curriculum designer. She conserves water by not showering every day. She doesn't mind being stinky for a good cause. She lives in San Diego with her very tall husband and very naughty dogs. To learn more about her, visit www.virginialoh.com.

# TABLE OF CONTENTS

# INTRODUCTION

Animals stink. They smell. They have **odors**. Odors are smells. Some animals make odors. They do this on purpose. They aim and fire. They squirt. They spray.

They spray for different reasons. They hunt. They protect themselves. They guard their area. They find things.

Some odors are **foul**. They don't smell good. They hurt **victims**' senses. They can blind. They can make victims sick. They confuse victims. Victims get harmed.

Some animals are extreme stinkers. Their stinks are bigger. Their stinks are better. They're the most exciting stinkers in the animal world!

Animals use odors to benefit them.

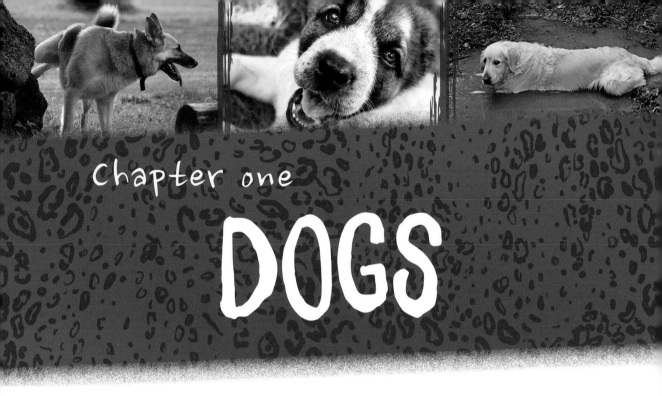

# Chapter one

# DOGS

Dogs like to roll around. They roll in anything. They roll in stinky things. They got this habit from wolves. Dogs came from wolves. Wolves roll in stink too. They roll in poop. They roll in guts.

Dogs leave messages. They pee. They poop. Their waste has odors. Dogs leave information about themselves. Male dogs mark. They pee. They guard their area.

Dogs can smell very well. They have long **snouts**. Snouts are mouths and noses. Snouts stick out. Their snouts are

*Dogs smell everything. They are picking up messages.*

super sensitive. They're a million times more sensitive than humans. Their wet noses trap odors.

# Chapter two

# VULTURES

Vultures are birds of **prey**. Prey are animals hunted for food. Vultures don't have sweat **glands**. Glands are organs. Glands ooze things. Vultures keep cool. They pee on their feet. They poop on their feet. This is better than sweating. It saves more energy. Their waste is smelly.

They have another reason for peeing. They need to clean. They have special pee. Their pee kills germs. They're **scavengers**. They eat dead animals. They walk on dead animals. Their pee cleans their feet.

Dead things have dangerous germs. Dead things can be

*Vultures rarely attack healthy animals. But they do attack sick and injured animals.*

deadly. A little bit of the germs can kill humans. A little bit can kill other animals. But vultures are fine. They have strong stomach juices. These juices kill harmful germs.

*A group of vultures eating is called a wake.*

Vultures can see and smell well. They can smell death a mile away. They fly. They look for dead animals. They quickly eat.

They have weak legs. Their claws are not sharp. But they have powerful beaks. They use their beaks. They rip apart dead animals. They help each other. They often eat in groups.

They dig with their heads. They dig into dead animals. They have bare heads. They have bare necks. This keeps them cleaner.

Many eat too much. They need to become lighter. Some vultures **vomit**. Vomit means to throw up. They do this so they can fly.

# HUMANS DO WHAT?!?

Human skin has more than two million sweat glands. These glands ooze water. They cool human bodies. They can be stinky. Armpits get sweaty. Germs live in this sweat. They create waste. Armpits get smelly. That's why humans use deodorants. There are people who smell armpits for a living. They have jobs as odor testers. Odor testers use their noses to help people. They improve and create products. Products are things people buy. People buy products to hide stinky body parts. People have smelly breath. Odor testers help develop mouthwash. Mouthwash is a special liquid. People rinse their mouths with the liquid. The mouthwash makes mouths smell good. People have many other smelly body parts. People have smelly rooms. People live smelly lives. Odor testers help develop all kinds of products. Odor testers smell the subject's body parts. Then the subject uses the product. Next, odor testers smell the body part again. They judge smells.

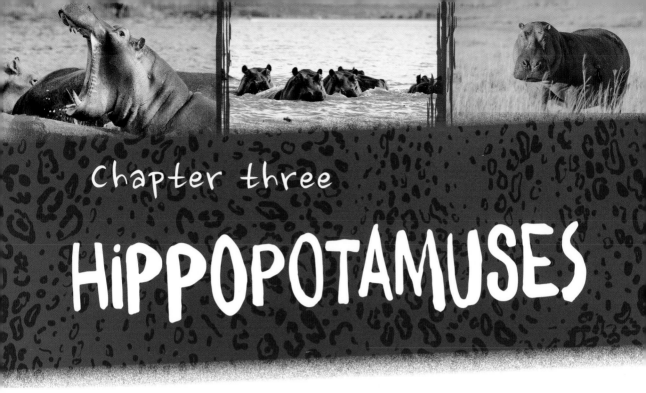

# Chapter three

# HiPPOPOTAMUSES

Hippos live in Africa. Male hippos show their strength. They do it in a special way. They spray **dung**. Dung is poop. It's called "dung showering." They show who's boss.

Hippos throw dung at victims. They spin their tails. Their tails spray dung. The dung goes all over the place.

Their dung is created by their **diet**. Diet is what they eat. They eat more than 100 pounds (45 kilograms) of plants. They eat this much every night. The food goes through their stomachs. It breaks down. It turns into a smelly soup. It becomes a stinky green mess.

*Hippos leave 9 tons of dung in the river each year.*

*Hippos can slice heads from shoulders in a single bite.*

Hippos do more than spray dung. They have more bite force than male sharks. They open their jaws wide. Their jaws open more than 4 feet (1.2 meters). Males have sharp teeth. Their teeth can be 28 inches (71 centimeters) long. They use their teeth. They block attacks. They attack.

They attack boats. They kill more humans in the wild than any other animal. They fight other hippos. They kill. They do it in one bite.

Hippos are very **territorial**. They guard their space. They protect their babies. Sometimes, they attack for no reason.

# DID YOU KNOW...?

- Bad smells release tiny molecules. Molecules are the smallest unit of a substance. They float through the air. They float up into noses. There are special little hair-like things at the top of noses. They catch odor molecules. That tells the brain that something bad is happening.

- Perfumes used to use substances from a musk deer's anal glands. The substance really smelled bad. So perfume makers had to dilute it. Dilute means to water it down. A tiny bit of musk made the other scents smell better.

- All humans make smells. Smells are part of natural body odor. Less washing releases more smells.

- Chemicals produced by some millipedes can burn or blister human skin. Don't touch millipedes!

- Some people keep skunks as pets. They remove the scent glands. One owner has eleven skunks. She said, "They're cuddly, quiet, and clean. They're very social animals." There could be up to 5 million pet skunks in the United States.

# Chapter four

# HOOKER'S SEA LIONS

Hooker's sea lions live in New Zealand. They live on the southern coast. They're the world's rarest sea lions.

They're super swimmers. They dive down over 1,500 feet (457 m). They hold their breaths. They can do it for 12 minutes. They hunt every day. They hunt underwater. They eat 60 pounds (27 kg) of fish a day. They live more than 20 years.

They don't clean their teeth. Fish get trapped in their teeth. The dead fish rot. Germs grow. Germs release stinky gases. These sea lions have bad breath.

*Hooker's sea lions' breath is caused by rotting dead fish and vomit.*

They have another stinky habit. Their bodies can't break down everything. Parts of fish can't be eaten. So these sea lions vomit.

# Chapter five

# HYENAS

Hyenas live in Africa. They live in **packs**. Packs are groups. They mark their territory. They cover the land. They mainly do this at night. They mark about 145,000 places each year.

They mark for different reasons. They keep other hyenas away. They guard their space. They're never more than 150 feet (46 m) away from their markers.

Their bodies have **anal** glands. Anal refers to the rear end. These glands make a stinky paste. It's called "hyena butter." It's powerful. It smells for up to 30 days.

*Hyenas communicate with smells.*

They also mark by pooping. Their poop is white. The white color comes from eating a lot of bones.

# Chapter six

# MUSKOXEN

Muskoxen smell of **musk**. Musk smells very strong. It is the smell of some animals. Some of these animals make musk. It comes from a gland.

Their name is tricky. First, muskoxen aren't oxen. They're shaggy. They're more like sheep. Second, muskoxen don't make musk. They don't have musk glands. Their musk is in their pee.

Males shower themselves with pee. They make a big stink. They smell musky. Their smell is so strong. It will make your eyes water.

*Muskoxen live in the Arctic. They're powerful land animals.*

They use their smell. They scare away others. They also fight. They butt heads. They have horns.

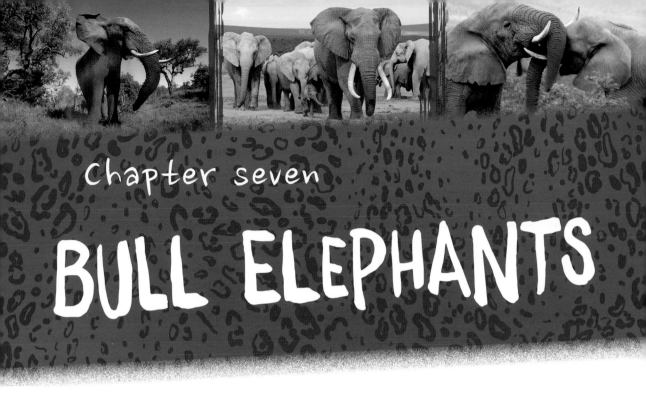

# Chapter seven
# BULL ELEPHANTS

Bull elephants are male elephants. They stink for one month each year. They go through **musth**. This means they're ready to mate. They make low rumbles. They make a thick substance. The substance is like tar. It comes from a small gland. The gland is on their heads. It's between the eyes and ears. The substance dribbles out. It smells really bad.

But females love the stink. They're attracted to the odors. Stinky means healthy.

Other males don't like the smell. They fight each other. Sometimes the loser dies. They're very violent. Elephants

*Bull elephants smell like 1,000 goats in a pen.*

live in herds. **Herds** are groups. Young males may get kicked out when they start smelling.

# chapter eight
# MiLLiPEDES

Millipedes live in forests. Most people think millipedes are harmless. But they're dangerous when they're in trouble. They create a big stink.

They mix two substances. They have mixing **chambers**. Chambers are like rooms. These chambers are on the side of their bodies. Millipedes make a deadly gas. The gas smells bad. The gas tastes bad.

Millipedes store the gas. The gas from one millipede can kill a mouse. The gas from 300 millipedes can kill a human.

*Millipedes have stink glands called ozopores.*

The deadly gas isn't easy to make. It takes a lot of energy. Millipedes would rather run than make it. They have hundreds of feet. But they're not fast.

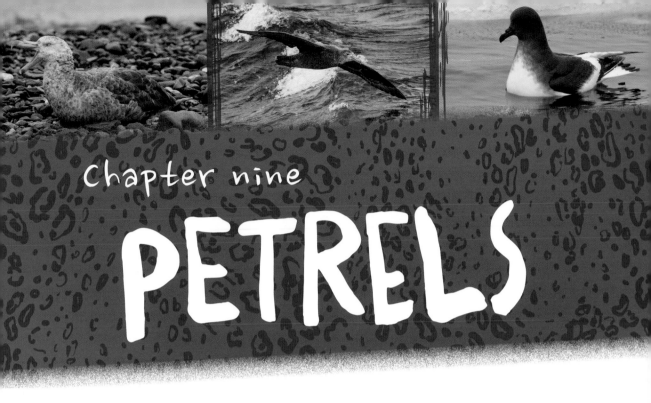

# Chapter nine

# PETRELS

Petrels are seabirds. They're big. Many live in Antarctica. Sailors call them "the stinkers."

They love to eat rotting flesh. They're the vultures of the southern seas. They're scavengers. They'll eat anything rotten.

They have another stinky habit. They aim and shoot with vomit. Their vomit is stomach oil. They spray **predators**. Predators are hunters. The vomit is very powerful. It smells gross. It makes things sticky. It doesn't wash out easily.

*Petrels have glands that filter salt. That means they can drink seawater.*

Their vomit affects other birds the most. It's bad for their feathers. It eats through the waterproof coating. It gets cooled by the air. It becomes glue. Bird feathers stick together. They become clumps. Then birds can't fly.

# chapter ten

# SKUNKS

Skunks scare off predators. They don't need to be big. They don't need to fight. They make one of the worst smells in the world. You can smell them 1.5 miles (2.4 kilometers) away. Skunk odors are harmful. They cause eyes to tear up. They blind eyes. The odors stick to victims. They attach to hair and wool. They mix with sweat. Victims stink for days.

Skunks have two anal scent glands. The glands are the size of walnuts. They're under their large tails. They're like powerful guns. They squirt up to 10 feet (3 m). They can only fire six times. They run out of stinky stuff. They make more. But it takes them 10 days.

Predators will only eat skunks
if other animals aren't around.

*Even baby skunks are smelly.*

Skunks know they have power. They're not scared. When in danger, they hiss. They stamp their feet. They turn around. They have good aim. They blast their victims.

There are different kinds of skunks. But they're all black and white. This alerts predators.

Skunks hunt at night. They eat plants, small animals, and insects. They also eat bees. They have thick skin. Their thick skin protects them. They don't feel stings.

They have powerful front claws. They smell well. They hear well. But they don't see well. They only see 10 feet (3 m) away.

# WHEN ANIMALS ATTACK!

Wolverines have glands that ooze oil. This oil smells musky. It doesn't smell good. It comes out like a large cloud. Wolverines are also known as "skunk bears" or "nasty cats." They spray to guard their space. They spray food. They bury their food to eat later. The smell helps them find the food again. It also keeps other animals away. They're tough. They have powerful jaws. They have sharp claws. They eat anything. Predators that attack wolverines from behind get stink-bombed. Victims can get blinded for several hours. They also smell bad. An Alaskan man was scared of a wolverine. He was trapped in the wild. He was cold. He was hungry. A wolverine stalked him. He said, "You could hear it on the ice, just playing with me, toying with me." He tried to shoot. But he ran out of bullets. He fought with a stick. He hid in a wooden box. He got rescued.

# CONSIDER THIS!

**TAKE A POSITION!** Some humans keep skunks as pets. They remove their scent organs. Do you think this should be allowed? Argue your point with reasons and evidence.

**SAY WHAT?** Stinky odors keep predators away. Explain how animals make stinky odors to survive.

**THINK ABOUT IT!** What are some ways that humans change the way they smell? Why do you think humans do this?

**LEARN MORE!**
- Artell, Mike. *Pee-Yew! The Stinkiest, Smelliest Animals, Insects, and Plants on Earth*! Tucson, AZ: Good Year Books, 2007.
- National Geographic—Five Animals with Stinky Defenses: http://voices.nationalgeographic.com/2013/09/19/5-animals-with-stinky-defenses/.

# GLOSSARY

**anal (A-nuhl)** rear end

**chambers (CHAYM-burz)** rooms

**diet (DYE-it)** what animals eat

**dung (DUNG)** poop

**foul (FOUL)** gross, not good, stinky

**glands (GLANDZ)** organs that ooze things

**herds (HURDZ)** groups of elephants

**musk (MUHSK)** strong-smelling substance from animals

**musth (MUHST)** bull elephants' time for mating when they emit a smelly substance

**odors (OH-durz)** smells

**packs (PAKS)** groups

**predators (PRED-uh-turz)** hunters

**prey (PRAY)** animals that are hunted for food

**scavengers (SKAV-uhnj-urz)** animals that eat dead animals

**snouts (SNOUTS)** mouths and noses that stick out

**territorial (ter-i-TOR-ee-uhl)** to be protective of an area

**victims (VIK-tuhmz)** subjects of harm

**vomit (VAH-mit)** to throw up

# INDEX